I0813184

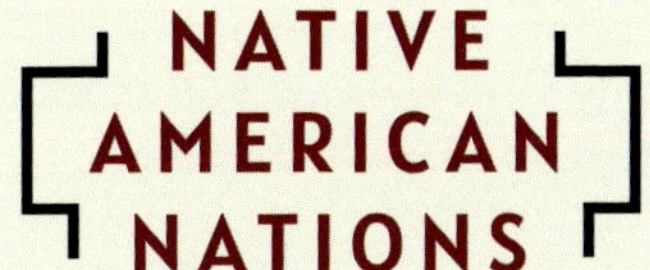

Shawnee

F.A. BIRD

Checkerboard Library

An Imprint of Abdo Publishing
abdobooks.com

ABDOBOOKS.COM

Published by Abdo Publishing, a division of ABDO, PO Box 398166, Minneapolis, Minnesota 55439.
Copyright © 2025 by Abdo Consulting Group, Inc. International copyrights reserved in all countries. No part of this book may be reproduced in any form without written permission from the publisher. Checkerboard Library™ is a trademark and logo of Abdo Publishing.

Printed in the United States of America, North Mankato, Minnesota
102024
012025

Editor: Lauri Nelson
Design: Mighty Media, Inc.

Cover Photograph: Albuquerque Journal/AP Photo
Interior Photographs: Ad_hominem/Shutterstock Images, p. 7; Angel Wynn/NativeStock, pp. 11, 13, 15, 17, 19, 23, 29; Bettmann/Getty Images, p. 27; EWY Media/Shutterstock Images, p. 25; Jim Lane/Education Images/Universal Images Group/Getty Images, p. 5; National Museum of the American Indian, Smithsonian Institution (2/6553, 2/9247, 2/486). Photos by NMAI Photo Services, p. 21; Stony River/Shutterstock Images, p. 9

Library of Congress Control Number: 2024938812

Publisher's Cataloging-in-Publication Data
Names: Bird, F.A., author.
Title: Shawnee / by F.A. Bird
Description: Minneapolis, Minnesota : ABDO Publishing, 2025 | Series: Native American nations | Includes online resources and index.
Identifiers: ISBN 9781098296254 (lib. bdg.) | ISBN 9798384917366 (ebook)
Subjects: LCSH: Shawnee Indians--Juvenile literature. | Pequea Indians--Juvenile literature. | Native Americans--Juvenile literature. | Indians of North America--Juvenile literature. | Indigenous peoples--Social life and customs--Juvenile literature. | Cultural anthropology--Juvenile literature.
Classification: DDC 973.0497--dc23

Contents

Homelands

The Shawnee homelands were located in what is now the northeastern United States. They lived east of the Mississippi River, along rivers such as the Cumberland and the Ohio. Their territory included parts of present-day Ohio, Tennessee, Kentucky, Virginia, and Pennsylvania.

The Shawnee homelands were beautiful. These lands held forested mountains, hills, valleys, and grasslands. Colorful wildflowers and flowering trees and shrubs covered the land. There were also lakes, streams, and ponds filled with fish, muskrat, and beavers, as well as many types of birds.

The Shawnee spoke a language in the Algonquian language family. In fact, the word *Shawnee* comes from an Algonquian word meaning "southerners." They lived south of other Algonquian-speaking nations. The Shawnee's neighbors included the Huron, Iroquois, Delaware, Kickapoo, and Miami tribes.

Cumberland Falls, on the Cumberland River, is the largest waterfall in Kentucky.

Society

The Shawnee built their villages along rivers. The rivers provided water to drink and food to eat. In addition, the rivers provided protection. For example, Shawnee villagers could use a river for a quick getaway when **hostile** people approached. For added protection, the Shawnee sometimes built a **palisade** around each village.

About 300 people lived in each Shawnee village. Originally, the Shawnee had 12 clans. The Shawnee were cared for by medicine people. These healers knew how to prepare herbs, wildflowers, tree bark, and other plants to cure illnesses.

Each village also had a peace chief and a war chief. Peace chiefs were responsible for setting up and performing ceremonies. War chiefs had the responsibility of protecting the village from hostile people. The chiefs worked together to plan hunting and fishing trips. They also acted as judges when villagers wronged each other.

THE SHAWNEE HOMELANDS
BRITISH COLUMBIA
ALBERTA
SASKATCHEWAN
MANITOBA
ONTARIO
QUEBEC
PRINCE EDWARD ISLAND
NEW BRUNSWICK
NOVA SCOTIA
Lake Superior
Ottawa River
St. Lawrence River
Lake Michigan
Lake Huron
Lake Ontario
Lake Erie
WASHINGTON
OREGON
CALIFORNIA
NEVADA
IDAHO
MONTANA
WYOMING
UTAH
ARIZONA
COLORADO
NEW MEXICO
NORTH DAKOTA
SOUTH DAKOTA
NEBRASKA
KANSAS
OKLAHOMA
TEXAS
MINNESOTA
IOWA
MISSOURI
ARKANSAS
LOUISIANA
WISCONSIN
ILLINOIS
MICHIGAN
INDIANA
OHIO
KENTUCKY
TENNESSEE
MISSISSIPPI
ALABAMA
GEORGIA
FLORIDA
SOUTH CAROLINA
NORTH CAROLINA
VIRGINIA
WEST VIRGINIA
PENNSYLVANIA
NEW YORK
MAINE
VERMONT
NEW HAMPSHIRE
MASSACHUSETTS
RHODE ISLAND
CONNECTICUT
NEW JERSEY
DELAWARE
MARYLAND
WASHINGTON, DC
Ohio River
Cumberland River
ALASKA
HAWAII
N
S
E
W
THE SHAWNEE HOMELANDS

Homes

The Shawnee made two common types of homes from natural materials. They built dome-shaped wigwams and rectangular bark houses.

To begin building a wigwam, Shawnee men first dug a pit 12 inches (30 cm) deep. This pit served as the floor. Next, men buried the ends of sapling poles in the ground. They bent the tops of the poles over the pit and tied them together to form a dome-shaped frame. Then the women covered it with animal **hides**, bark, or mats woven from cattail reeds. An opening was left in the side for a door.

The second type of home was a bark house. This home also began with a frame of sapling poles. The men covered the frame with bark, then tied cross poles to the frame to hold the bark in place. In the roof, they left a smoke hole.

Both types of homes had doors of either woven mats or animal hides. Inside, the Shawnee made beds by covering branches with hides or fur robes.

Shawnee men covered their rectangular houses with either elm or birch bark.

Food

The Shawnee produced their own food. They hunted, fished, and gardened. They also gathered wild plants. Some of the plants they gathered were wild leeks, berries, nuts, and herbs.

Shawnee men hunted with flint-tipped spears and bows and arrows. For meat, they hunted elk, bison, and deer. They also set traps to catch rabbits, squirrels, beavers, ducks, and geese. Shawnee men fished for bass, walleye, catfish, pike, perch, and muskellunge. To catch the fish, the men used spears and a hook and line.

Shawnee women grew corn, beans, squash, and sunflowers. The Shawnee ate many of the crops while they were still fresh. But, they also dried some vegetables, meat, fish, and wild plants in the sun and saved them to eat during the winter. Ripe corn was dried and ground into **meal**. The meal could be used to make corn bread or mush.

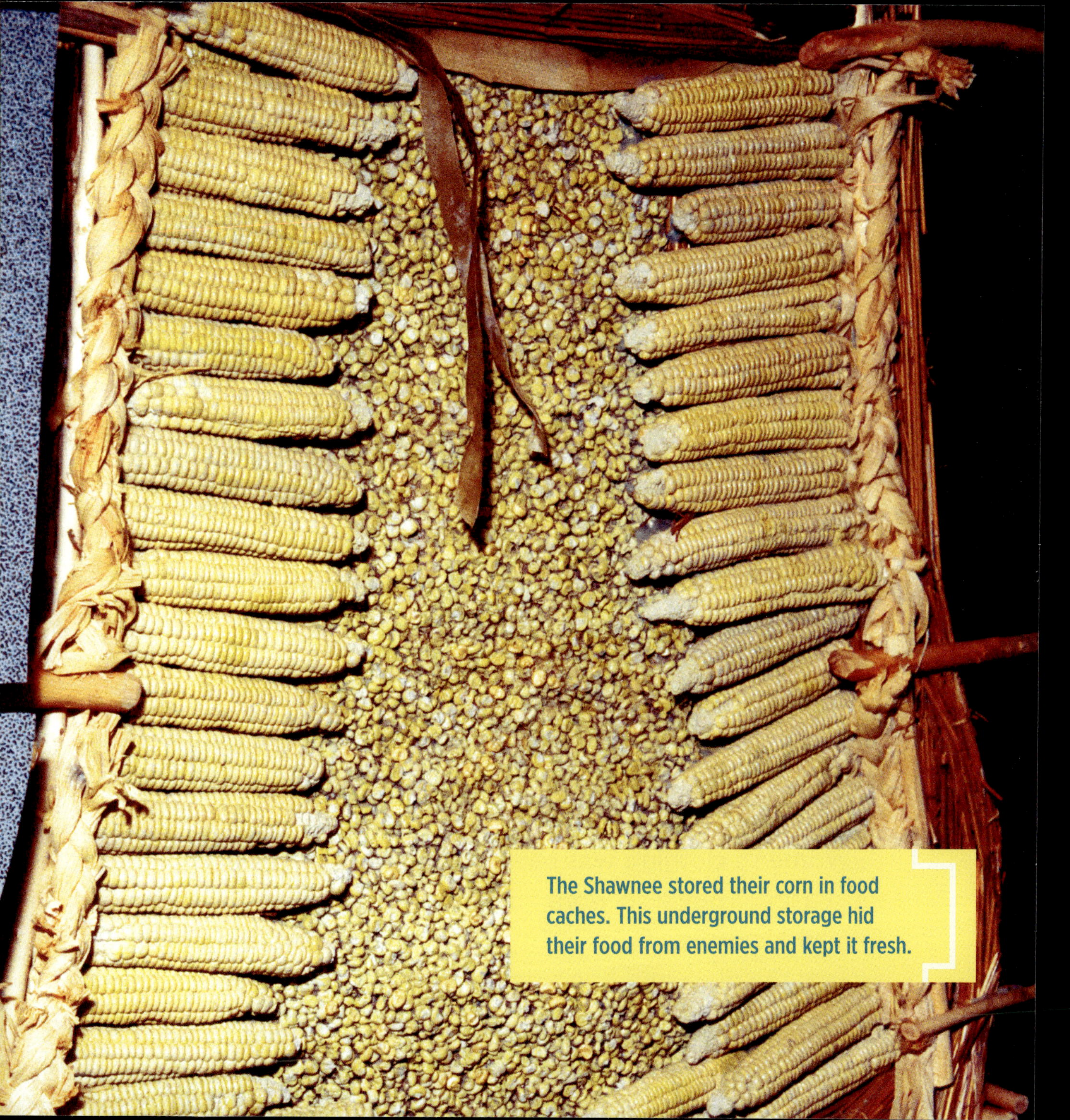

The Shawnee stored their corn in food caches. This underground storage hid their food from enemies and kept it fresh.

CHAPTER 5

Clothing

Women made the Shawnee's clothing. They sewed with bone needles and thread rolled from plant fibers or animal **sinew**. They made the clothes with plant fibers or deer, elk, or bison **hides**. Once done, the women decorated the clothing with porcupine **quillwork** or paint.

Men's clothing consisted of animal-skin **breechcloths** and moccasins. They wrapped sashes and belts around their bodies. Men also wore **leggings**. The leggings protected their legs from brush and thorns.

On their heads, Shawnee men wore turbans or wide headbands. They often decorated the turbans with a feather. Feathers from eagles, hawks, and owls were highly respected.

Women's clothing was usually deerskin dresses and moccasins. They also wore animal hides and skirts, as well as mantles woven from plant fibers. These mantles tied around the neck and hung down to the top of the skirt.

Traditional Shawnee clothing includes a frock shirt, leather leggings, and a roach headdress. The roach is often made from the tail hair of deer.

CHAPTER 6

Crafts

The Shawnee were skilled craftspeople. One common craft was making birch bark containers. They used bark because its inner layers are strong. To begin a project, the Shawnee used stone, bone, or antler tools to cut strips of bark from a tree.

Next, they soaked the strips in water to make the bark soft and flexible. Then, the Shawnee cut the bark and bent it to form bowls, plates, baskets, and other containers. Finally, they punched holes into the sides and sewed the pieces of bark together with spruce roots.

Besides making bark containers, the Shawnee also carved. To prepare, they first took maple or oak **burls** and heated them in a fire. Heating the burls made them easier to carve. Then, they carved the burls into bowls and cups.

The Shawnee also made pottery. Their pots had round bottoms and sturdy, ridged necks. They carved a simple design of straight lines into the ridged tops of the pots.

Shawnee birch bark basket and lid decorated with porcupine quillwork

CHAPTER 7
Family

Shawnee villages were made up of extended families. Family members worked together to feed and protect the people of the village. The Shawnee gathered wild berries, greens, sunflowers, and medicinal plants. In addition, they collected hickory nuts and walnuts. The Shawnee also gathered some plants to make natural dyes.

Shawnee women tended the gardens. They planted corn, beans, pumpkins, and melons. While the people worked, Shawnee elders helped watch the children. They also taught the children by telling them stories.

Men fished the rivers, lakes, and streams. Shawnee men also went on hunting trips. Sometimes they traveled great distances to find bison herds on the prairie. When they returned, the men built drying racks. The women cut strips of fish or meat and hung them on a rack to dry. Sometimes they placed the rack over a fire to smoke the meats.

Children used a stick platform to scare birds away from crops and to store freshly picked food.

Children

The Shawnee love their children. After a baby's birth, a Shawnee family named their child during a special naming ceremony. The parents chose the name from the father's clan. Babies were carried on **cradleboards**.

Shawnee children had a great knowledge of nature. Shawnee territory was home to poisonous snakes, including cottonmouths and timber rattlesnakes. The Shawnee taught their young children how to identify and avoid these dangerous snakes.

Boys and girls learned by helping with daily village tasks. Boys learned how to make stone, bone, and antler tools. They watched as the men chipped away stone to make spears and arrowheads.

Shawnee girls helped the women plant and weed the gardens. The girls also learned how to make clothing. They practiced by sewing dresses and tiny moccasins for their dolls.

A young dancer in his regalia. A dancer's powwow regalia is worn with responsibility and pride. The outfit is a collection of items that displays their lives, interests, and family background.

Traditions

Every Native American nation has its own creation story. These stories tell how the people came to this world. The following is a Shawnee creation story.

A long time ago, there was no planet Earth. There was only a Sky World, and beneath this world was nothing but clouds and water. One day Kuhkoomtheyna, "Our Grandmother," left Sky World. She sat on a cloud and created a giant sea turtle. She placed the sea turtle in the water.

Next, Kuhkoomtheyna began to create the earth. She made streams, rivers, mountains, valleys, meadows, and lakes. She also made trees, birds, and animals.

Kuhkoomtheyna placed the earth, which looked like a giant ball, on the turtle's back. Then she created her grandchildren, the Shawnee and other peoples. She gave the Shawnee fire and medicine bundles, and she taught them ceremonial dances and songs.

Shawnee buffalo headband, gourd rattle, and wooden flute used in special ceremonies

CHAPTER 10

War

The Shawnee often had to fight to protect themselves. They fought against many Native American nations. The war chiefs planned how to launch an attack on the enemy. These leaders also trained the young warriors.

In warfare, the Shawnee fought with bows and arrows. For close combat, they used stone, bone, or antler knives. They also fought with two kinds of war clubs.

The Shawnee crafted root war clubs from the root close to a sapling tree. They carved the knobby roots to make them sharp. Ball war clubs were made using a **burl** from a maple or oak tree. The men attached handles carved from ironwood trees to the burl. Sometimes they embedded a tooth or arrowhead in the burl to make it more deadly.

When Shawnee traded with Europeans, they got guns and metal knives. But, many enemy tribes received these goods before the Shawnee. As a result, many Shawnee were killed, and those remaining were forced to new lands.

A ball war club was used for hand-to-hand combat in battle.

Contact with Europeans

The Shawnee's early contact with Europeans was friendly. In the late 1600s, French explorer René-Robert de La Salle explored the Ohio region and the Mississippi River. Some of this land was Shawnee territory. At one point, one of his men joined and lived with a band of Shawnee.

But, in the early 1770s, the British colony of Virginia took lands belonging to the Shawnee. Traders and settlers soon moved into these areas. Some Shawnee launched raids against the settlers. The Shawnee were defeated.

During the American Revolution, the Shawnee fought with the British against the colonists to stop the American colonists from settling in their territory. In 1795, the Shawnee and other tribes signed the Treaty of Greenville with the United States. This treaty caused the Shawnee to lose a lot of their original homelands.

Monument in Maumee, Ohio. The Battle of Fallen Timbers in 1794 was the final battle of the Northwest Indian War.

CHAPTER 12

Tecumseh & the Prophet

Tecumseh (tuh-KUHM-suh) was a respected Shawnee leader. He was born in about 1768 in present-day Ohio. His brother named Tenskwatawa was known as the Prophet. The two men worked hard to protect the Shawnee people.

At this time, it was common for individuals to sell lands that did not belong to them. Tecumseh and the Prophet wanted the people to agree that land could not be sold without approval from all of the Native nations. Tecumseh said that if the nations united, they could stop the loss of land and **culture** due to the US westward **expansion**.

During the War of 1812, Tecumseh fought on the side of the British. He hoped the British would stop the settlers from invading Shawnee lands. Tecumseh died at the Battle of Thames on October 5, 1813, in present-day Ontario, Canada.

The name *Tecumseh* means "Panther Springing Across the Sky."

The Shawnee Today

In 1830, the US government created the Indian Removal Act. The purpose of the act was to remove Native American tribes from their homelands and relocate them west of the Mississippi River. The US government relocated the Shawnee to present-day Oklahoma.

Today, there are three **federally recognized** Shawnee tribes. Their reservations are all in Oklahoma. The Absentee Shawnee includes the Big Jim Band and the White Turkey Band. They have an elected government and an Elder's Council. The Elder's Council plans social activities.

The Eastern Shawnee tribe is working to improve the lives of its members. For example, it is working on a housing development for its members, and it promotes Eastern Shawnee businesses.

The Loyal Shawnee govern their people through a Tribal Council and a Business Council. They have a goal for all Shawnees to use their traditional language in daily life.

Ceremonial dances are a way for the Shawnee to protect their language and culture.

Glossary

breechcloth—a piece of hide or cloth, usually worn by men, that is wrapped between the legs and tied with a belt around the waist.

burl—a hard, rounded woody growth on a tree.

cradleboard—a flat board used to hold a baby. It could be carried on the mother's back or hung from a tree so that the baby could see what was going on.

culture—the customs, arts, and tools of a nation or people at a certain time.

expansion—something made larger.

federal recognition—the US government's recognition of a tribe as being an independent nation. The tribe is eligible for special funding and protection of its lands.

hide—an animal skin that is often thick and heavy.

hostile—unfriendly.

leggings—coverings for the legs, usually made of cloth or leather.

meal—coarsely ground seeds.

palisade—a fence of strong stakes placed closely together and set firmly into the ground.

quillwork—the use of porcupine quills to make designs on clothing or cradleboards.

sinew—a band of tough fibers that joins a muscle to a bone.

ONLINE RESOURCES

To learn more about the Shawnee, please visit **abdobooklinks.com** or scan this QR code. These links are routinely monitored and updated to provide the most current information available.

Index